Camping Adventure

by William R. Gray

Photographs by Steve Raymer

☐ BOOKS FOR YOUNG EXPLORERS
NATIONAL GEOGRAPHIC SOCIETY

A family hikes
past a pond
high in the mountains.
Dave, Rob, and Cindy
are going camping
with their parents.
For a few days,
they will live outdoors.
They are carrying
everything they need
in their big backpacks.
They will see no cars
or TV.
But they will see
many beautiful things.
And they will find
many things to do.

Everyone becomes hungry and thirsty while hiking.
Dad takes a sip of water as he walks.
Later, the family stops in a sunny spot for a picnic lunch.
The food tastes very good after the long hike.
Dad rests before he puts on his heavy backpack again.
Hikers must have a lot of rest.
They must be sure to carry plenty of food and water, too.

The family has found a good camping place, near a lake.
The children help their father put up a tent.
The tent will keep them warm and dry at night.

Rob fills a bucket at the lake. Mom will use the water to cook dinner.
Soon it is bedtime, and Cindy brushes her teeth.
Everyone is tired but happy. It has been a long, busy day.

Wake up! It's a good day to go exploring.
Dave stretches his arms out of his warm sleeping bag.
The ground feels a lot harder than a bed!
Dave pulls on thick socks.
Then he laces up his hiking boots.
After breakfast, the children watch as their father
pours water on a campfire.
He is careful to put the campfire out
because he doesn't want to start a forest fire.

Which way will they go today?
The family uses a map to help plan a hike.
The map shows where to find mountains, lakes, and streams.

The family decides to climb high in the mountains.
Soon they reach a rocky stream.
Mom and dad help Cindy across.
The family stays close together.
They know it is not safe to hike alone.

Stones keep
the map from
blowing away.

Rob and Dave look at the side of a big rock.
They see something that looks like spots of paint.
What is it? It feels rough and flaky.
Mom tells them that it is a plant called a lichen.
Lichens are tiny plants without leaves that can grow on rocks.
Nearby, in a meadow, the boys find red and yellow wild flowers.
The boys do not pick the flowers. They leave them for others to see.

CINQUEFOILS

COLUMBINE

LICHENS

Surprise!
Snow in the summer.
The boys find a snowfield.
It's fun to jump
and slide on the snow.

The snow is left from winter.
In the high mountains
there are places
where the snow never melts.
Cindy makes a snow cone
with an orangeade mix.
Her tongue feels so cold.

It gets chilly in the mountains at night, even in the summer.
A campfire and hot cocoa chase away the cold.
After a day of hiking and exploring, everyone is hungry for a hot dinner.
Mom cooks on a small camp stove.
Dad likes the way dinner tastes.
Cleanup comes next. All the washed cups are hung on a branch to dry.

Here comes a hungry bear.
It is looking for food.
Sometimes bears steal food from people.
Bears are strong, dangerous animals
and should be left alone.

The family knows how to keep bears
away from the food.
First the family puts the food in sacks.
Then Rob and Dad use a long rope
to pull the sacks high up in a tree.
One day, Dave has fun
swinging on a rope.

Deer live in the mountains, too.
A young mule deer
stands quietly in a meadow.
With its big ears, it can hear many sounds.

The deer will stop to feed on some bushes.
But if it hears a loud noise,
it will run away quickly.
It won't stop until it feels safe,
deep in the woods.

A ground squirrel nibbles on a flower.
These squirrels live in homes underground.
For their homes, they dig holes, or burrows.
If a ground squirrel is in danger,
it runs down its burrow and disappears.

That tickles!
Cindy laughs
as her father
rubs her foot
during a rest stop.
The family stops to rest
often while hiking.
While Rob rests,
he looks around.
He sees the mountains
sparkling with snow.
All around the family
hundreds of
tiny wild flowers dot
the meadow.
It is peaceful and quiet.

Cindy and her father look closely at a rock.
They use a magnifying glass.
Up close, they see many tiny specks of color.
Later that day, the family finds a pond.
They look down into the water and see frogs and insects.
Then they dip their cups into the water to see what else they can find.
Cindy catches a tiny insect and puts it in a plastic box.
After watching it swim around, she puts it back in the pond.

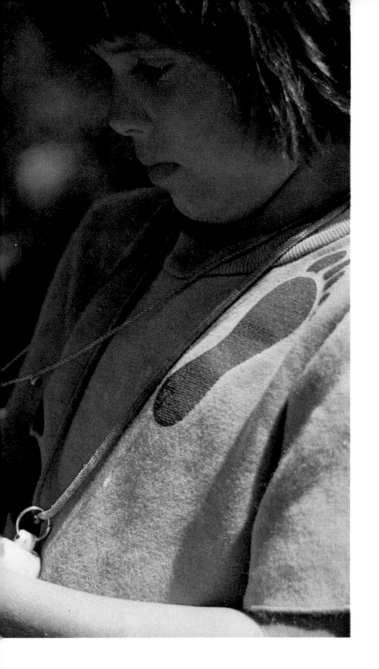

One afternoon,
the family goes fishing.
At first, Dave catches his sleeve
instead of a fish.

Soon the children catch some trout.
They take turns cleaning the fish.

Now the fish are ready to be cooked.
Mom will fry them on the stove.

Dave and Rob crawl
under a big mosquito net to play.
They are also trying to get away
from mosquitoes. Sometimes there are
many mosquitoes in the mountains.
Before supper, Rob plays his harmonica.
Dave rests as he swings in a hammock.

At dusk,
Rob takes a short walk.
He carries a flashlight
and stays close to camp.

In just a few days,
he has learned to be
a safe and careful camper.
He has also enjoyed
the beauty of the outdoors.
With his brother, sister,
and parents, Rob now feels
at home in the wilderness.

Published by The National Geographic Society
Robert E. Doyle, *President;* Melvin M. Payne, *Chairman of the Board;*
Gilbert M. Grosvenor, *Editor;* Melville Bell Grosvenor, *Editor-in-Chief*

Prepared by
The Special Publications Division
Robert L. Breeden, *Editor*
Donald J. Crump, *Associate Editor*
Philip B. Silcott, *Senior Editor*
Cynthia Russ Ramsay, *Managing Editor*
Susan C. Burns, *Research*

Illustrations
David R. Bridge, *Picture Editor*
Josephine B. Bolt, *Art Director*

Production and Printing
Robert W. Messer, *Production Manager*
George V. White, *Assistant Production Manager*
Raja D. Murshed, June L. Graham, Christine A. Roberts, *Production Assistants*
John R. Metcalfe, *Engraving and Printing*
Jane H. Buxton, Stephanie S. Cooke, Mary C. Humphreys, Suzanne J. Jacobson,
Marilyn L. Wilbur, *Staff Assistants*

Consultants
Dr. Glenn O. Blough, Peter L. Munroe, *Educational Consultants*
Ed and Linda Best, *Story Consultants*
Edith K. Chasnov, *Reading Consultant*

Illustrations Credits
All photographs by National Geographic Photographer Steve Raymer except
Len Lahman (18 top and bottom, 26 bottom right, 29).

Things to take when you go camping:

1. tent; 2. tent pegs; 3. binoculars; 4. plastic bottle for water; 5. map; 6. compass; 7. toilet paper;
8. first-aid items; 9. lip balm; 10. sunscreen; 11. wool cap; 12. raincoat; 13. hat with brim; 14.
backpack; 15. sleeping bag; 16. down parka; 17. fuel for portable stove; 18. cooking spices; 19.
energy foods; 20. pocketknife; 21. drinking cup; 22. wooden matches; 23. freeze-dried food; 24. foam
pad to go under sleeping bag; 25. soap, toothpaste, toothbrush; 26. groundsheet; 27. sleeping bag;
28. towel; 29. thermal underwear; 30. extra plastic bottle; 31. flashlight; 32. whistle; 33. waterproof
matches; 34. wool mittens; 35. lightweight socks; 36. heavyweight wool socks; 37. shoes for around
camp; 38. tee shirt; 39. down booties; 40. hiking boots; 41. bandanna; 42. lightweight shirt; 43. sack
for sleeping bag; 44. wool shirt; 45. hiking shorts; 46. rugged trousers.

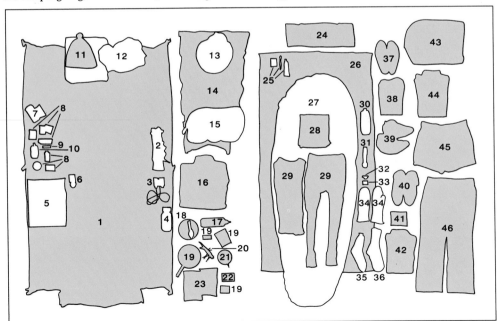

Things to take when you go camping.